THEY TRIUMPHED OVER THEIR HANDICAPS

THEY TRIUMPHED OVER THEIR HANDICAPS

BY JOAN HARRIES

Franklin Watts

New York | London | Toronto | Sydney | 1981

A Triumph Book

To George with love

Photographs courtesy of Wide World: pp. 5, 48, 50, 52, and 72; United Press International: pp. 13, 18, 46, 58, 62, 66, 69, 82 (top and bottom), and 84; Atlantic Records: pp. 14, 21, and 24; Jay J. Armes: pp. 27, 28 (top and bottom), 35, 39, and 40; Jeffrey R. Werner: p. 43; *Friends Magazine*: p. 80.

R. L. 2.5 Spache Revised Formula

Library of Congress Cataloging in Publication Data

Harries, Joan.
They triumphed over their handicaps.

(A Triumph book)
Includes index.
SUMMARY: Profiles the lives and achievements of six
severely handicapped people who triumphed over blindness, deafness, missing limbs, and brain damage to excel
in sports, music, jobs, and living optimistically.
1.   Handicapped—United States—Biography—Juvenile
literature.   2.   United States—Biography—Juvenile
literature.   [1.   Physically handicapped]   I.   Title.
CT9983.A1H3   362.4′092′2 [B] [920]   80-25016
ISBN 0-531-04267-7

CONTENTS

Johnny-No-Legs—Skydiver

1

*Ray Charles Brings Back
the "Good Old Days"*

11

Meet Jay J. Armes, Private Eye

26

*Kathy Miller Came in
Among the Last—and Won*

42

Ted Kennedy, Jr.—Runner-Up

56

*Kitty O'Neil—
Fastest Woman on Earth*

71

Index

87

I appreciate the assistance given to me by the following while I was doing research for this book: Ted Mayfield; Lyle Bowman of the Tahlequah Public Library, Tahlequah, Okla.; Sheridan Public Library, Sheridan, Oreg.; U.S. Parachute Association; Shirley Watson of the El Paso Public Library, El Paso, Texas; Lawrence J. Bowman of the Scottsdale Public Library, Scottsdale, Ariz.; Marie Payne, Ms. O'Neil's companion and secretary; Margaret Jean Owens of the Glendale Public Library, Glendale, Calif.; and particularly the Oak Park Public Library, Oak Park, Ill.

I am very grateful to Ray Puechner for his help and encouragement.

And special thanks to my husband, George Katsarakis, and our daughter, Louise Katsarakis, for helping me in many, many ways.

In this book you will read about
a skydiver, a singer, a private eye,
a runner, a skier, and a rocket-car driver.

One is blind. One has no legs.
All six have serious
physical disabilities, or handicaps.

The rocket-car driver has
set world records. The skier was
runner-up for a sports award.
In a 10,000-meter race, the runner
came in among the last.

These six show us that
people don't have to win to be winners.
But they have to try.

All these people have tried.
All have triumphed.

JOHNNY-NO-LEGS-SKYDIVER

Ted Mayfield runs a parachute center in Sheridan, Oregon. While I was doing research for this book, he wrote me a letter. Here is part of what he said:

"It was in 1975. I was parachuting in Tahlequah, Oklahoma.

"A man I know brought a fellow over to me. The man said, 'Ted, this is Johnny Fry. Will you train him to make his first parachute jump?'

"I couldn't believe my eyes. There sat a young man. He looked about twenty-two. He had a big smile—and no legs.

"My first thought was NO. I didn't say anything, but a lot of questions came into my mind. I wanted to ask this Johnny-No-Legs how he intended to land. If he meant to land on his back, he'd break it. Also, the harness holds the jumper and the chute together. With no legs, how could he hook up the leg straps? And how could he get

1

out of the plane? A person has to have feet to stand on the step. Finally, how would he stand up against the wind?

"I still didn't know what to say. I went on thinking, 'Sure, if you make a good jump, you and I'll be great. If you don't, my neck will be as far out as it will go.'

"At last, I found a way out. I knew what to say. I told Johnny, *no way* could I train him at Tahlequah. But in Sheridan, I could have a special harness made. I could give him special training. I'd train him if he'd come to Sheridan, Oregon—a thousand miles away.

"That'll fix Mr. Johnny-No-Legs," I said to myself. "That's the last I'll hear of him.

"Two weeks later in Sheridan, my phone rang. Johnny Fry. He said, 'Ted, I'm here in Sheridan. At the bus station. Can you pick me up?'

"He had hitchhiked all the way from Oklahoma.

"I knew then that nothing would stop Johnny. He was going to jump.

"The next Monday Johnny was to begin

2

training. All of us at the center were shaking. We asked ourselves, 'How's he going to land?'

"Johnny showed us. He landed on his hands. No problem.

"A young girl, Diana Leslie, was working for me. She spent hours training Johnny. First, he practiced PLFs off a platform. [A PLF is a Parachute Landing Fall.]

"Johnny was quick and good at everything. But Diana had him do each part of the training over and over. She wanted to make sure.

"After one week the harness was ready. It was built like a basket. Johnny sat in it. He buckled it in front.

"He was going to make his first static-line jump. In a static-line, a line goes from the plane to the parachute. The jumper doesn't open the chute. The static line opens it.

"I was Johnny's jumpmaster. I would be in charge of him from the time he got in the plane until he got out.

"I was just as excited as he was. We had decided not to use the step. I held him out on the

3

wing strut [the bar between the body of the plane and the wing]. He let himself go.

"It was one of the nicest first jumps I'd seen in a long time. I felt great. I knew Johnny did too.

"There was no way he could carry his chute and walk at the same time. So a motorcycle took him back to the parachute loft.

"The news got around. Soon everybody in Sheridan knew. Johnny-No-Legs had made his first static-line jump!

"After that, Johnny made about ten more static-lines. He was ready for freefall. Freefall is the big leap. There's no line from the plane to open the chute. Johnny would pull the ripcord himself.

"Johnny jumped. The crowd cheered. TV news cameras took pictures. Other jumpers ran to him. They shook his hand. Johnny was the first skydiver with no legs!

John Fry (left). Standing beside the plane is flight instructor Cecil Hammonds.

"You can be sure there was a big party in Sheridan that night!

"Johnny meant to hitchhike home. The Sheridan people said no. They bought him a first-class ticket. They said, 'Be sure to stay in the plane, Johnny. No jumps.'"

Mayfield finished his letter: "There will always be a special bright spot in my heart for Johnny-No-Legs. He's as complete as any of us— I guess even more so."

By now Fry has jumped thirty-three times. Why does he do it? Wouldn't it be easier to stay home and watch TV or play cards or *anything*? Sure, but John wasn't brought up to look for the easy way.

John was his parents' first child. He was born without legs.

The doctor told them, "Don't baby this child. Teach him to do things for himself."

It took lots of time, lots of patience. But they helped John find his own way of doing things. When it was time for him to walk, he did—on his hands.

Four sisters and a brother were born. They

learned from their big brother that a handicap can stop you—but only if you let it.

John's father was a sergeant in the United States Air Force. He and Mrs. Fry lived in England when John was born. Because of Sergeant Fry's work, the family moved around a lot. John went to school in England and all over the United States. Every time he went to a new school, he had to get used to new children.

And they had to get used to him. At times this was hard. Most of the kids had never before seen anyone without legs. They stared. They kept away. But after a while they found out John was okay. That is, most of them found out. To a few kids, John seemed like a great person to pick on. He didn't have legs. He couldn't fight back.

That's what *they* thought! In every school, John had to beat up a few kids. He had to show them he could take care of himself. John's arms were powerfully strong. They had to be. They had to do the work of arms *and* legs.

John didn't like to fight. He tried to keep away from troublemakers. But when he had to fight, he did.

John said, "When I was a kid, I hated when people stared at me. I hated to be different.

"Now, I know I *am* different. I am proud to be Johnny-No-Legs. I am proud to show people I can do things.

"When kids see me on the street, they say, 'Hey, mister, what happened to your legs?' I like that. Kids with active, healthy minds want to know things."

One thing that gets Fry down is when people want to keep him from trying. *Parachutist* is a magazine put out by the United States Parachute Association. It says that Ted Mayfield was just about the only skydiver who didn't say, "Go talk to someone else, kid. You can't jump without legs."

Sometimes, when Fry has applied for jobs, they've said to him, "Sorry, Mr. Fry. We have steps. You'd fall." They've said this to a man who jumps from planes.

Fry told a writer for the newspaper *Tulsa World,* "A few times I've felt like giving up. But I guess that happens to everyone. Sure, some things take a little longer for me to learn. I keep trying until I get them right."

He went on, "Of course, I'll never be a basketball star. But if I want to do something bad enough, I almost always find a way."

Fry found a way to scuba dive. He hopes to get his black belt in karate. He holds a blue belt now.

Because his father was in the air force, John grew up around planes. He likes them. So, two months after he learned to skydive, he took up flying. He has special pedals in the airplane he uses. He controls them with a touch of his finger. The pedals fit any single-engine plane. He has special pedals for his car too.

In eight months Fry had his private pilot's license. Now he's working for his license to *teach* flying.

When John's father retired from the air force, he said to John, "What about college? If you go, I'll go too."

So both of them went. They went to Northeastern State College. Mrs. Fry wasn't about to be left out. She went too.

John's father studied industrial technology. He learned about tools and machines. Now he works in electronics for the telephone company.

Mrs. Fry learned how to teach children who have special problems. She teaches children who are mentally retarded.

John studied sociology. He learned about people and how they get along together in groups.

He graduated in 1978 and married a girl named Theresa. Theresa went to Northeastern also. She was studying special education. Like her mother-in-law, she wanted to teach children who have special problems.

John and Theresa have a son named William.

John went back to school to study psychology. He wanted to help people find out why they think, feel, and act the way they do.

When Fry has his master's degree, he would like to help handicapped children. Or maybe he will work in a mental hospital or prison. He wants to help people learn to go after what they want. They mustn't let anyone or anything stop them. They can triumph over their handicaps.

I told Fry I was writing this book. He said, "Tell your readers *I* can do things. So can *they.*"

RAY CHARLES BRINGS BACK THE "GOOD OLD DAYS"

The good old days are here again. Young and old alike are hounding the stores for records by Elvis, the Beatles, and the Beach Boys.

Rock 'n' roll is back. The Big Bands are back. Jazz is bigger than ever.

And so is Ray Charles! Ray's broad shoulders, big smile, and dark glasses are often seen today on television and in the theater. Ray is performing in concert halls too.

Teenagers today sway to "How Long Has This Been Going On?" It's from Charles's hit album, *True to Life*. Their parents swayed to his first hit, "I Got a Woman."

Ray Charles was the first to play what later was called "soul." Soul is gospel music, the blues, and jazz put together. From about 1955 to 1965, Charles was called Soul Brother Number One. Today's music makers have him to thank for many of the sounds they're producing.

11

Charles started out big among black people. Later, his moans and whoops and laughs made him the Giant of the Music World. Frank Sinatra was the first to call Charles, "the Giant."

Charles was born in Albany, Georgia, on September 23, 1930. He was named Ray Charles Robinson. Later, he dropped the "Robinson." He didn't want people to mix him up with the boxer, Sugar Ray Robinson.

Ray's parents moved to Florida when he was a few months old. They had another child, George. George was two years younger than Ray.

Their father's name was Bailey Robinson. Bailey worked for the railroad. He had to be away from home a lot. He cut and mended crossties.

Ray's mother was named Aretha. She cooked and did other housework for white families. She worked at a sawmill sometimes too.

Ray Charles,
born Ray Charles Robinson
in Albany, Georgia.

Ray Charles says, "Soul is a way of life—but it is always the hard way."

Charles has known the "hard way" ever since he was very young. When he was four, he and George were playing in their front yard. Aretha's washtub was there. It was full of water. George fell in.

Ray tried to pull him out. George was too heavy. Ray ran to get his mother. It was too late. George had drowned.

When Ray was five, something went wrong with his eyes. They began to secrete fluid. He had pain behind them. He could not see well.

Ray's mother didn't have the money to take Ray to a specialist. The doctor in the town did what he could. He told Ray to stay out of bright lights. He gave him drops to put in his eyes.

The drops didn't help. By the time Ray was seven, he was blind. Doctors now tell him he must have had the disease glaucoma. Glaucoma happens when the fluid of the eyes can't drain into

Ray Charles recording for Atlantic Records.

the surrounding blood vessels. A specialist might have been able to prevent Ray's blindness.

Some blind children take a long time to adjust. Not Ray. His mother wouldn't let him sit around. "You're blind, not stupid," she told him. "You've lost your eyes, not your mind."

Aretha taught Ray to scrub floors and sweep them. She taught him to chop wood. She told him that someday she would not be there to help him. He'd have to do things for himself. He'd better learn now.

Aretha had not had much schooling herself, but she taught Ray the alphabet. She taught him to print. She taught him a little arithmetic too.

And Ray learned about music. He learned about it from Wylie Pittman. Pittman had a café near Ray's home.

There was a piano in the café. When Pittman played, Ray came running. Sometimes Pittman would let Ray bang on the piano. He would tell Ray how well he played.

By the time Ray was seven, he could play a few tunes. He liked to sing too.

The Robinsons sent Ray to the State School

for the Blind in St. Augustine, Florida. There he learned Braille, which is a way of writing and printing. It uses raised dots. Blind people can read by touching these dots.

The state paid for the childrens' bus fare to the school in September. It paid for the bus fare home in June. It did not pay for visits home at Christmas.

Whitney Balliett wrote in *The New Yorker* magazine on March 28, 1970, "Charles said, 'Somehow my mother always got the money. I remember leaving at Christmas, and there would be two or three kids left at school who wouldn't get home. I didn't want to leave them there alone. I also wanted to see my mother.' "

Ray did well in music at the school. He played pieces by the great masters—Chopin, Mozart, Bach, Beethoven. He liked knowing how to play what they wrote.

When the teacher left the room, Ray played jazz. He took more freedoms with jazz. He could experiment, play it as he pleased.

When Ray was fifteen, his mother became ill. The doctor said it was because of something she'd

Ray sings a duet with
Glen Campbell on television.

eaten. She died the next day. She was only thirty-three.

Ray came home from school. He couldn't cry. He couldn't eat. After some weeks, a woman neighbor had a talk with him. She told him his mother would not want him to give up like that.

For the first time since his mother died, Ray cried. Then he remembered her words, "You'll have to do things for yourself."

Mr. and Mrs. Thompson had been friends of Ray's mother. They asked him to stay with them. He said he would. He wanted to pay them. He earned money by playing the piano at parties. But they wouldn't take any money.

He stayed with the Thompsons about six months. Then he went to Orlando, Florida. He got a job. It was with a sixteen-piece band. He sang. He did arrangements. He would imagine how the music should sound. Then he'd call out the notes for each instrument. Someone in the band would write the notes down for him.

Of course, Charles's ear for music was sharp. Play a wrong note and he'd know it.

Charles trained his ears to do what his eyes

19

couldn't. He would stand in an enclosed hallway and throw a golf ball. He'd listen to the sounds it made. Then he'd try to catch the ball as it bounced back to him.

Charles's band didn't get many jobs. At times, Charles had to live on beans, crackers, and water.

Charles told a writer for *Ebony* magazine in October 1974, "Times and me got leaner and leaner, but anything beat getting a cane and cup and picking out a street corner."

Some people told Charles he couldn't sing. They told him he sure couldn't play. He didn't give up. He says now that he always believed in himself. He knew he could be successful.

Things got better. He saved some money. He wanted to travel. So he took out a map. Seattle, Washington, was as far from Florida by bus as he could go. So he went to Seattle.

He got there at five in the morning. He slept twenty-one hours straight. Then he woke up and

Ray relaxes at home in his office.

asked where he could hear some music. He was told about a club. It was called the Rocking Chair.

Once there, Ray asked the manager to let him sing. He sang "Driftin' Blues." The manager liked Charles's singing and gave him a job.

He got other jobs. He met Louise and they fell in love. In the book *Brother Ray,* by Ray Charles and David Ritz, Charles says, "Even though Louise and I have gone our different ways with families of our own—I still have the feeling that spark between us is something which will never completely die." Ray and Louise have a daughter, Evelyn. She is grown now and is studying to be a nurse.

Later, Ray married Della Beatrice. He got some musicians together. He formed his own band. His first big hit was "I Got a Woman." It was the start of soul, or rhythm and blues, in America.

Charles was a success. But he began to take drugs. The law caught up with him. He went to a hospital for help. Eventually he got free of drugs. But it wasn't easy. And he lost a year of work. After he was through with drugs, though, big hits came one after another. Charles was a millionaire by the time he was thirty. He won awards—all the top ones in the music world.

In 1964, Dave Dexter, Jr., wrote a book called *The Jazz Story*. In it he called Charles the "Kingpin among male jazz singers."

Today, Charles shares the spotlight with other musicians. Some of his personal favorites are Barbra Streisand, Frank Sinatra, Aretha Franklin, and Stevie Wonder. His favorite jazzmen are Dizzy Gillespie, Oscar Peterson, and Clark Terry.

Charles heads two firms that publish music. He and Della Beatrice have three sons, Ray, Jr., David, and Robert.

But success in the music world has brought problems too. After being married twenty years, Ray and his wife were divorced. In *Brother Ray,* Charles says, "Far as my family went, music proved to be a blessing and a downfall." He made money but it kept him away from a normal home life.

Charles still remembers seeing some things such as sunsets, the moon, and his mother. But he makes a point of not looking back. He told writer

Whitney Balliett, "There are so many things you can see without the eye. . . . I know what this desk is like and what this chair is like and what a woman is like. . . . And there are things I don't want to see, like people lying in the street. . . . I know what my kids look like to me. I suppose that if there was anything in the world I really wanted to see before I die it would be them."

In *Brother Ray*, he tells us that sometimes he hears his mother's voice comforting him, telling him that the world isn't all that bad. "There's pain, there's joy, and there's a way to deal with both," said Aretha. Ray has learned to deal with both. He has triumphed.

MEET JAY J. ARMES, PRIVATE EYE

Jay J. Armes is a private investigator. Some people say he's the best private eye in the world.

Armes keeps a gun in his Rolls-Royce. It's a submachine gun. It's always kept loaded. Armes is a man of peace. But at least thirteen times people have tried to kill him. Now, he takes no chances. His life is too good to give up. He has a wife, Linda. He and Linda have three children.

Jay J. Armes also has everything money can buy. He has eight cars in addition to his $37,000 Rolls-Royce. He has two planes. And he owns a million-dollar house. It has an indoor swimming pool and gym. The gym cost $90,000.

Behind the house are the family tennis courts. Next to them is the landing pad for the helicopter.

Then there is the zoo. Armes owns some panthers, a tiger, a puma, and a chimp.

Finally, there's a lake with a waterfall.

Jay J. Armes seems to have everything—ex-

Jay J. Armes keeps all his limousines
fully equipped for his work.

cept hands. His hands were destroyed when he was thirteen years old.

He was born Julian Armas in Ysleta, Texas. Later, he changed his name to Jay J. Armes. His mother, father, two sisters, and two brothers made up his family. His father worked in a grocery store.

Even as a young boy, Julian went full speed. When he was eleven, he got up at 4:30 every morning. He delivered newspapers. After that, he fed sixty calves for a farmer. He fed them from bottles.

Then he went to school. By the time he got out, the afternoon newspapers were waiting for him. And the calves needed their bottles again.

After supper, Julian went to the movie house. He had two jobs there. He was an usher and he took tickets.

For a while, Julian was a loanshark. At the beginning of each week, he'd lend quarters to kids

The famous detective likes to play tennis on his private court and relax with his family near the "zoo."

at school. When they got their allowances, the kids would have to pay Julian fifty cents for each quarter they had borrowed. Sometimes Julian would have to fight to make them pay up.

The principal found out. He made Julian promise to stop lending money in school.

Julian kept his promise. He went on loan-sharking but across the street. It was a great way to make money, he thought. Now, he knows how wrong it was.

Julian had a friend who was a doctor. This doctor loaned him books. He answered Julian's questions. He even let Julian watch him sometimes when he operated.

Julian made up his mind. He would be a doctor. He wanted to operate, so he decided to be a surgeon.

He didn't make it. One evening he was in his backyard. It was May 1946. Julian was thirteen years old. A friend, Dickie, came to Julian's yard. Dickie was eighteen. He brought a box with him.

Dickie told Julian that there were railroad torpedoes in the box. Railroad torpedoes are put on railroad tracks. When the wheel of a train runs over them, they explode. The noise warns that the train is coming.

The boys used an icepick to open the box. Julian took something out. Dynamite. Two sticks exploded in his hands.

The explosion blew Julian about 20 feet (6 m). He fell to the ground, face down.

He tried to help himself up by grabbing a tree. He couldn't. His hands were in bloody pieces.

Dickie drove Julian to a doctor. The doctor put tourniquets on Julian's arms to stop the bleeding. He gave him a shot to kill the pain. Then he took him to a hospital.

There, his hands were amputated.

Julian had only one thought. He wanted to die. His family did all they could, but nothing they did or said helped him. Julian just kept asking himself, "Why did this happen to *me?*"

Then one day he decided he was being selfish. He must stop thinking only about himself.

Frederick Nolan wrote a book about Armes. It is called, *Jay J. Armes, Investigator.* When

Nolan was writing it, Armes told him, "I've never felt sorry for myself since that day, never felt that I got a rawer deal than the next man."

The head of the Ysleta public schools, F. W. Cooper, said he'd never seen a boy change as much as Julian. Cooper spoke to Virginia Turner, who was writing for the El Paso *Herald-Post*. "After this accident Julian seemed to make up his mind he would not let it be a handicap. He was never sorry for himself. He was always cheerful."

Doctors operated on Julian's arms, so he could have steel hooks to replace his hands. The doctors made a tunnel in his biceps. Biceps are the large muscles in the upper arms. They are the muscles you can see when you try to "make a muscle" in your arm.

The doctors put a "pin" through each bicep. The pins make the hooks work.

Julian had a hard time learning how to use the hooks. He had to train his biceps. He had to make them much stronger than before.

And he had to learn all over again things he'd learned when he was a little kid. Tying his shoelaces was a big job. Buttoning his shirt was too. And so was writing his name. But he kept on trying.

Julian relearned how to ride his bicycle. Then he got a motor scooter. He learned how to tie newspapers and throw them from the moving scooter. He fell down a lot. But each time he picked himself up and tried again.

One thing was easier for him—fixing his scooter. Hooks can get in places that fingers sometimes can't.

Julian had a pair of artificial hands too. But he used these only for "dressing up."

Armes says there's another good thing about hooks. When he used to come into the house, his mother would say, "Wash your hands." Hooks put an end to that.

Butch was Julian's two-year-old German shepherd. Until Julian learned to use his hooks, Butch did many jobs for him. Opening doors was one.

At first, Julian hated when people saw his hooks. He told a reporter for the *El Paso Times,* "When I first got my hooks, I thought I couldn't stand to have people stare at me all the time. But I soon got used to it. Now I don't mind the staring."

In high school, Julian made the baseball, basketball, and boxing teams. He had dates.

"You are handicapped only if you think you are," he said.

He graduated from high school.

He thought he'd like to be a movie star, so he went to Hollywood. He stayed there six years. He didn't become a star. But in those six years he had small parts in thirty-six movies and twenty-eight TV shows.

Directors liked his big build, black hair, and smile. But one director told him his name didn't sound good for the movies. That's when Julian Armas became Jay J. Armes.

Armes decided he didn't want to be an actor all his life. So he went back to school for a degree in criminology. He wanted to learn why some people get into a life of crime. After Armes got his degree, he headed back to Texas. He knew what he wanted to be. He wanted to be an investigator.

Getting started wasn't easy. Armes rented

*Armes with Jack Lord in an episode
of television's "Hawaii Five-O."*

an office in El Paso. He hired a secretary. He hired ten agents. But then, he tells us, "Nothing happened. I wasn't even asked to find a lost dog."

He learned he'd better go to the people. He couldn't afford to wait for them to come to him. He went out looking for people who needed help. He paid for radio ads.

He found people who had been robbed. Some of them felt the police weren't doing enough to find the robbers and the stolen goods.

He found people whose children had run away from home.

The people looked at Armes's hooks. Some thought he couldn't do the job.

Armes told them, "If I take your case, I will stay on it all the way down the line. If I don't solve it, I won't charge you a cent."

Soon Armes had more work than he could handle. He caught shoplifters. He caught robbers. He found missing wives, husbands, children, friends, and lovers.

More and more people called on him. He solved cases for kings and presidents. He did jobs for Elvis Presley, Frank Sinatra, and Elizabeth Taylor.

Armes calls his cases "capers." They got tougher and tougher. But, Armes tells us, he has never had a caper he couldn't solve.

He did a job for Marlon Brando. This caper was reported in newspapers all over the world.

The actor's thirteen-year-old son, Christian, had been kidnapped. Armes found out the kidnappers had been driving a red Volkswagen bus. They had driven to Mexico.

Armes followed them there. He rented a Hughes 500 helicopter. For four days he looked for the red VW. He went without sleep and food. He almost crashed his chopper once but pulled it up just in time.

He found the VW and Christian. He had to hold eight kidnappers at gunpoint to make the rescue. But he got Christian safely back to Brando.

Armes has been shot in the chest at close range. He shot back with his concealed .22 magnum pistol. A surgeon had built the controls for this pistol into Armes's right arm. The pistol is hidden in his right hook. He can fire the gun by moving a certain muscle.

Armes isn't telling us what's built into his *left* hook. He says it's his "$100,000 surprise."

He doesn't know who rigged his Corvette Stingray. It was booby-trapped with a single-barreled shotgun. The gun was aimed to shoot right at Armes's belly the moment he entered the car.

But Armes didn't enter. He saw that someone had been fooling with the car.

Armes is always alert, always watching out. That's why he's still alive.

His armed bodyguard goes everywhere with him. Closed-circuit TV takes care of his house and family. The cameras are on the job all the time.

Armes is a crack shot with every kind of gun. He practices shooting an hour every day. He does this in a concrete bunker under his house.

He spends another hour every day working out in his gym. He does karate exercises. He lifts weights. He does *1,800* pushups a day. Using hooks has made his arms strong!

Armes taking target practice
in his underground bunker.

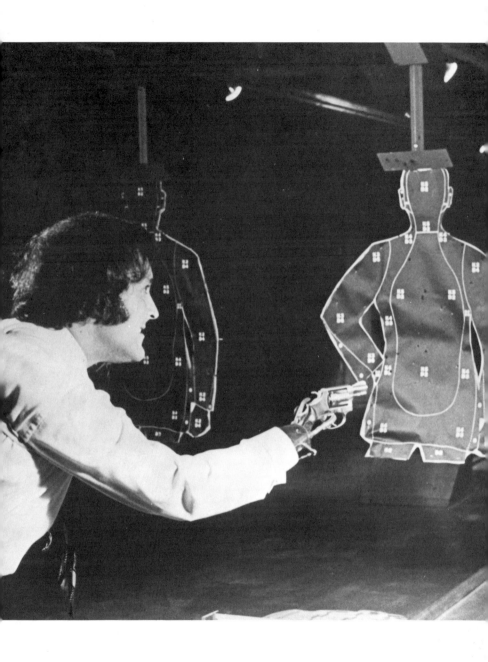

In his book, Armes says he is not trying to break records or prove anything. He's just trying to get everything he can out of life. "The more I draw on myself," he says, "the more I find I have left."

He can smash plate glass with his fist. He can pry apart the links of a steel chain. He can pick up a red-hot blowtorch.

Armes isn't handicapped. He doesn't have hands. But that's not stopping him from much of anything.

Armes practices karate using a punching bag.

41

KATHY MILLER CAME IN AMONG THE LAST-AND WON

Thirteen-year-old Kathy Miller of Scottsdale, Arizona, had high hopes. She wanted to swim in the Olympics. She wanted to be a long-distance runner.

Already she was a good runner and a great swimmer. She was also a cheerleader and a straight-A student.

Kathy's father, Larry, was a pitcher in the 1960s. He pitched for the Dodgers and the Mets. He and his wife, Barbara, knew Kathy was a winner. Anyone could tell that just by looking at her. She was beautiful—blonde and freckled. And she was full of life. She was always in a hurry to do things, go places.

On March 14, 1977, Kathy was rushing to meet friends at a favorite hangout. She ran across a four-lane highway. The speed limit was 50 mph (80 kmph).

Brakes squealed. There was a thud. Kathy

had been hit—head-on. The car spun around and around. Kathy's body was on the hood.

Kathy was rushed to the hospital. One leg was crushed. And her brain had been badly injured. She couldn't hear, see, or feel. She was in a coma.

"It's a miracle she's still alive," the doctors said. "Most likely she'll die. She'll never come out of her coma."

But Kathy did. Ten weeks later, she woke up.

Before the accident, she weighed 110 pounds (49.5 kg). When she came out of the coma, she weighed 50 pounds (22.5 kg). She was like a baby. The doctors thought she might stay that way the rest of her life. They told Barbara and Larry to put Kathy away in an institution. She would be taken proper care of there.

Kathy couldn't talk or walk. She had no control of her body. She had to wear diapers.

Barbara and Larry knew that sometimes love can do what doctors can't. Early in June they took their daughter home.

They started teaching her. They tried to make her feel she could do things.

First, she had to learn to crawl. It was a big day for the Miller family when Kathy was able to drag herself along the floor.

Saying a word was Kathy's next triumph. She began to write. She took her first steps.

Over and over, Barbara and Larry told her, "With God's help, Kathy, you can do anything you want."

The third week after Kathy came home, she was talking. Sometimes it was hard for her to get the words out. And when she did, people didn't understand her. So Kathy tried again and again.

By the middle of July, Kathy was walking. She fell lots of times. But she'd pick herself up and go on.

Once in a while she couldn't help thinking of all the things she used to do. Now, even going up stairs was a hard job. And she had trouble remembering things, too.

Her mother said, "Look ahead, Kathy. Think of all the good things you're *going* to do."

One day Barbara asked Kathy, "What one thing do you want to do more than anything else?"

"Run," said Kathy.

*Kathy with her
mother and brother.*

Barbara brought out Kathy's jogging outfit. Kathy began.

Jogging was slow work at first. But little by little Kathy did better.

In the March 3, 1979 issue of *Sporting News*, Bill Lyons tells us, "By the end of August she was running. Well, not exactly running." He goes on to say that Kathy went to a quarter-mile track with her parents. She'd go forward quickly on her good leg. Then she'd drag the broken leg after her. It took her forty-five minutes to go the first quarter of a mile.

Three weeks later she was still trying to run evenly, smoothly. But her nerve centers were all mixed up. They didn't give the right messages to her muscles. So the muscles couldn't do their jobs properly.

Kathy fell down lots of times. Once she fell on her face. Her mother tells us, "Kathy was a bloody mess." Her nose was broken. Her eyes were swollen shut. Her parents took her to the doctor.

"I don't think I should operate on her nose yet," the doctor said. "Let's wait a while and see what happens."

Kathy's nose healed by itself. The doctor said, "I don't know what there is about you, Kathy Miller, but everything seems to heal."

On November 6, Kathy ran in a 10,000-meter marathon in Phoenix, Arizona. Her parents ran too, so they'd be with Kathy if she needed help.

Kathy and her parents were among the last to finish. But it was a triumph. As Kathy said later, "I didn't run to win. I just ran to finish."

After that, Kathy ran in a girls' cross-country meet. She finished third out of seventy-five. Her father said, "Eight months ago it was beyond our wildest dreams that Kathy could be here today."

News of Kathy's bravery reached sports people all over the world. In February 1978, she won the International Valor in Sports Award. It was given to her by Prince Michael of Kent at the Great Hall of London.

Prince Michael is a cousin of Queen Elizabeth

Kathy runs with her parents, training for a 10,000-meter race.

49

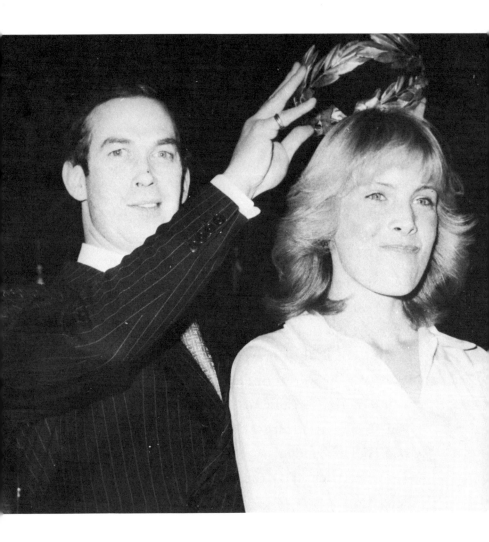

*Britain's Prince Michael of Kent places the
winner's wreath on Kathy's head. Kathy won
the International Valor in Sports Award for 1978.*

II of England. He placed the winner's wreath on Kathy's head.

In ancient times, Greek and Roman winners were crowned with leaves of the laurel tree. That's why Kathy's wreath was laurel leaves. But her laurel was made of gold.

Kathy thanked Prince Michael. She thanked her family. Then she said, "Most of all I'd like to thank the good Lord for, you know, keeping me alive and helping me through it."

Kathy spoke slowly and carefully. She wanted to make sure her words came out right.

Later she said, "I was terribly excited to think I'd won."

Waiting to shake Kathy's hand was pop singer Elton John. He's a sports fan. He said that meeting Kathy was one of the high points of his life. "She's a beautiful lady from a beautiful family. They are all a great credit to the United States."

While Kathy was in Britain, she went to Belfast, Northern Ireland. She ran around a track with Mary Peters. Peters is a 1972 Olympics winner. She won the women's pentathlon gold medal. The pentathlon has five different events, includ-

ing the broad jump, the javelin throw, the 200-meter sprint, and the 1,500-meter run.

Peters was one of the judges for the valor award. She said Kathy had a good chance of being a top runner. "There's a man here who lost both his legs and still climbed the Matterhorn. So who dares to say Kathy won't make the Olympics?" asked Peters.

Being in the Olympics sounded great to Kathy. But when she got back to the United States, she changed her mind. She told Pat McElfresh of the *Scottsdale Daily Progress*, "I really just like to jog, to trot along."

That was fine with Kathy's parents. They don't want Kathy to feel she has to be super-woman. They know that sometimes "just trotting along" is a triumph.

Kathy went to special education classes at Scottsdale High School. After school, she'd sit at

After receiving the award,
Kathy chats with singer Elton John.

the electric typewriter in the kitchen. A lot of people from all over the world had written to her. She pecked out answers to all of them. She signed each one. This was not easy for Kathy. Her muscles don't always do what she wants them to. And she had to get used to writing with her left hand. Before the accident, she used her right. But now that hand shakes.

Kathy still has trouble with words. Sometimes she can't remember the one she wants and has to ask for help. She goes to Scottsdale Christian Academy. She's not a straight-A student anymore. She has to work hard to get Bs and Cs. She studies three or four hours a day. Her father told sportswriter Bill Lyons, "A lot of mornings I'll get up at six and she'll be already at the kitchen table doing her homework."

The Philadelphia Sportswriters Association named Kathy The Most Courageous Athlete of 1978. But, as Lyons says, "Don't get the idea that such a triumph of courage has come easily. Kathy Miller has been through hell."

Kathy says, "There are times I'll get mad when I can't do something I remember I used to do so easily and take for granted. But if you say a prayer and just hang in there, things will turn out okay."

Things are turning out okay for Kathy Miller. She's fifteen. She's back to her 110 pounds (49.5 kg). She's full of life.

And she helps others whose lives are not okay right now. She works with High Hopes. High Hopes is a group that helps people whose brains have been damaged.

Kathy visits hospitals. She tells people that if she can do things, they can too. She thinks that sometimes people give up too soon. She tells them, "Hang in there."

TED KENNEDY, JR.—
RUNNER-UP

Ted is twenty years old. He's smart, and he goes to the best schools.

He has traveled—to China, Russia, France. It's hard to name all the places he's been.

Ted is good-looking. He has good-looking parents. They're rich. And they love him. So do his brother and sister.

Ted has lots of cousins. They sail, swim, and boat together.

Kids like Ted. So do adults.

It would seem as though Ted's life were perfect. But there's another side to it.

When he was little, Ted's mother and father were away from home a lot. He missed them.

And he was scared. He still is. He had two uncles he loved. Both were shot and killed.

Ted's afraid his father will be shot too. His mother is afraid of the same thing.

Ted and his family have been through a lot. In 1964, Ted's father was almost killed in a plane crash. In 1969, he had a young woman with him in his car. They were coming home from a party. The car went off a bridge. The woman drowned.

Ted's mother for many years had a drinking problem. She and Ted's father were separated for long periods of time.

When Ted was twelve, he got a lump on his leg—cancer. The leg had to be amputated.

Ted has known the best of life and the worst.

Who is Ted? He's Edward M. Kennedy, Jr., the son of Joan and Edward M. Kennedy. Both he and his dad are called "Ted."

Ted's father is a United States senator. Young Ted's uncle was President John F. Kennedy. President Kennedy was assassinated in 1963. Ted was two years old.

Senator Kennedy tried for the presidency himself in 1980. Ted was fearful. His Uncle Jack was President when *he* was killed. His Uncle Robert was trying to become President when *he* was killed.

From 1961 to 1964, Robert F. Kennedy was Attorney General of the United States. Later, he

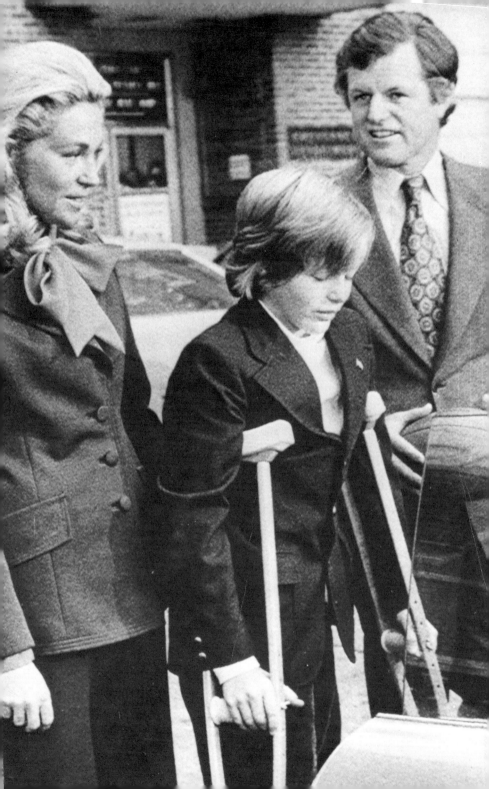

was a senator. He was killed in 1968. Ted was seven.

Whenever his father was away from home, he'd phone Ted every night. That way Ted knew his dad was okay.

But there was fun for the Kennedys too. Ted loved sports. He liked camping best of all.

When Ted was twelve, his mother went to Europe. His father took him on a vacation to Colorado. Three of his father's friends went too, with their three sons. They had a great time riding the rapids on a raft in the Colorado River.

One day in November, Ted didn't feel well. He had a fever and a cold. He stayed home from school. His father was at work.

Ted was sitting up in bed watching TV when Theresa came into his room. Theresa took care of

Twelve-year-old Edward M. Kennedy, Jr., leaves the hospital under his own steam, only two weeks after his leg amputation.

the Kennedy children when their mother and father were away.

Theresa saw a lump on Ted's leg. "What's that?" she asked.

Ted looked at the lump. "I think I got it playing ball."

The lump was about 3 inches (7.5 cm) below Ted's kneecap. It felt hard.

As soon as Senator Kennedy came home, he called the doctor.

The doctor thought the lump was just a bruise. But he wanted to make sure. When it didn't go away in a few days, Ted was checked into the hospital. His leg would have to be X-rayed.

Ted's mother came home from Europe as fast as she could.

Ted had the X-ray. Then he had more tests. The doctors found out he had a kind of cancer that spreads quickly. It had to be operated on right away.

Later, Senator Kennedy said that telling Ted his leg had to be amputated was one of the hardest things he had ever had to do. Ted cried. So did Senator Kennedy.

The next morning Dr. George Hyatt cut

through the skin and muscles of Ted's right leg. He cut just above the knee joint, through the thighbone. He drew the muscle and skin ends over the bone. This would pad the stump.

Then Ivan R. Sabel went to work. Sabel is a bioengineer. He fits people with artificial limbs.

Sabel put a plaster cast over what was left of Ted's leg. This cast would stop the cut from swelling. With no swelling there would be less pain.

The plaster cast was used as a base for Ted's artificial leg. The leg itself was made of aluminum. The foot was molded rubber. The foot and leg were Ted's prosthesis.

Sabel put the prosthesis on Ted right away. Until 1963, a person whose leg was amputated had to wait months before getting a prosthesis. The swelling had to go down. The cut had to heal.

Now, people can be fitted with prostheses before they leave the operating table. They can walk sooner and don't feel so much pain.

And, it is much better to wake up after an operation and see something under the sheet that *looks* like a leg, even though it's not real.

Ted woke up and saw the prosthesis. He

61

made a face. But he knew he had to make the best of it.

The next evening he sat up in bed. He swung both legs over the side. He stood up. He said it didn't hurt much.

For a few weeks, Ted said he felt pain in the leg that had been cut off. The nurse told him this was normal. Most people who have a limb amputated feel that way. It's "phantom" pain. It soon goes away.

Good Housekeeping magazine, in October 1974, said that two weeks after his operation Ted was ready to walk. He was wheeled into another room. Dr. Hyatt was waiting. Dr. Covalt was there too. He was going to help Ted get used to his new leg.

"All right, Ted," Dr. Covalt said. "Let's stand up."

Ted held on to the arm rests of his chair. He leaned forward. He lifted himself. He made him-

Ted and his father on a fishing trip.

self let go of the chair. It would be so easy to give in to fear, to pain.

But that way, he'd never play ball again. He'd never ski. He'd be in a wheelchair the rest of his life.

Ted stood up. He took a step. Dr. Covalt said, "He was shaky, but he never shed a tear. He was also scared to death. Anybody would be. But he did as he was asked. That took courage."

When Ted stepped down on the new leg, it hurt. But he walked. He walked to the bars at the end of the room. He took hold of them. He looked back—and grinned. The doctors sat him in his wheelchair and took him back to bed.

Dr. Covalt said, "He's a gutsy kid. He's got what it takes."

The first leg was only a temporary one. About four weeks after his operation, a permanent leg was ready. Its knee was made of metal and wood. Because it had joints, it would bend like a real knee. This leg would be easy for Ted to put on and take off.

The leg part was made of plastic. The foot was molded rubber. The whole prosthesis weighed 7.5 pounds (3.37 kg). It cost $1,000.

At first Ted walked with crutches. Before long, he was riding a bike with three wheels. The crutches were in the wire basket behind him. By the end of the winter, he didn't need crutches any more.

After the hospital, Ted spent a few weeks at home. Then he went back to school. And he joined his cousins and friends in camping, sailing, and bike riding.

Geraldo Rivera, in his book *A Special Kind of Courage,* tells us Ted started skiing again on beginners' slopes. A special ski was fitted to his prosthesis. He'd ski, slide, then fall down the hillside. He kept telling himself he'd skied before. He'd learn again.

At last he was able to come down alone. A reporter asked, "How's your leg doing?"

Ted looked back at the slope. He said, "I just don't think about it much."

Every month Ted had to return to the hospital. He was receiving chemotherapy treatments. Chemotherapy involves taking drugs to fight disease. It helped prevent Ted's cancer from coming back.

Ted had to lie still with a needle in his arm

for six hours. Medicine from a bottle overhead dripped into his bloodstream. By evening he would feel sick. But the next day he would feel all right again.

Once Ted went on a trip to Ireland. He went with five other boys and an adult. While he was in Ireland, he got bad news. His mother had been admitted to a psychiatric hospital. She needed help with her emotional problems.

Ted also got sick from his chemotherapy treatment. He had had the treatment before he left the United States. Most of the time he reacted right away to the drugs. This time he didn't react until he was on vacation.

His father flew over to Ireland to be with him. In a few days, though, he was fine again. He and his dad went fishing.

Ted loves to fish. But he knows work too.

Ted makes one-legged skiing look easy on this run down a slope in Vail, Colorado.

When he was thirteen, he and two friends went to his father's office. They asked for a job.

Senator Kennedy put them to work sorting mail.

That was boring. After a while, the boys began chasing each other around the desks. They threw paper wads at each other. They shot rubber bands.

By the time Ted was fifteen, he was a better worker. He worked in a parking lot.

The next summer he wanted something more exciting. He looked around. At last he and a friend got a job on a cruise ship.

The ship stopped in Israel and Egypt. Ted was surprised when "little kids ran up to me and touched my leg. They'd never seen anything like it." He added, "Legs like mine are made to last a lifetime. I go through one a year."

That's no surprise. Ted skis, swims, scuba

Ted here congratulates the winner of the 1979 International Valor in Sports Award. Ted was the runner-up.

dives, climbs rocks, lifts weights, and sails. For some sports, like scuba diving, he takes the artificial leg off.

In the spring of 1979, Ted and his father went to London. There, Ted was honored as the runner-up of the 1979 Valor in Sports Award.

Ted didn't win the big prize. That went to a man from Japan. The Japanese man had traveled to the North Pole alone over the ice of the Arctic Ocean. He had also climbed some of the world's highest peaks.

Ted hasn't reached the North Pole. He hasn't climbed the highest peaks. But he has fought pain, fear, and self-pity—and certainly triumphed.

KITTY O'NEIL–
FASTEST WOMAN
ON EARTH

The man dragged the woman to the edge of the roof. She looked down at the street—six stories below. She kicked and clawed and screamed.

It was no use. The man was going to throw her down.

The woman's foot slipped. Her body twisted. She fell.

But she grabbed the ledge of the roof. She hung there. How long would it be before she'd drop to her death?

Robert Blake saved her just in time.

The cameras stopped rolling. The woman brushed her dark-brown hair back from her face. The day's work was done for Kitty O'Neil, stunt woman. She was working as a double for actress Lana Wood. They were filming an episode for TV's "Baretta."

Did you ever watch "Baretta"? Or "Bionic Woman"? Or "Police Woman"? Or "ABC Super-

Look again. It's not Wonder Woman. Or is it?
It's Kitty O'Neil, substituting for Lynda Carter
in an episode of the TV show "Wonder Woman."

stars"? If so, then you've probably seen Kitty O'Neil.

Or maybe you've seen her in movies. She was in *Airport '77* and *Omen II*.

O'Neil was in *9/30/55* too. This was the story of James Dean's death. Do you remember when the oil lamp tipped over? Lisa Blount's cape caught fire. But that wasn't Lisa Blount in the cape. It was Kitty O'Neil. She takes over for the stars when things get rough.

O'Neil has always looked for action. As a teenager, she was an Olympic-class diving champion. In 1970, she set a world's record for women's water-skiing.

On December 4, 1976, she drove a rocket car to become the Fastest Woman on Earth.

Kitty O'Neil is 5 feet 3 inches (1.58 m) tall. She weighs 95 pounds (43 kg). And she is deaf.

It's partly because she's deaf that O'Neil is a champion today. Ever since she was little, she has had to struggle to get what she wanted.

Kitty was born in Corpus Christi, Texas, on March 24, 1946. Her father was Major John O'Neil of the United States Army. He was a Marauder.

The Marauders were tough jungle fighters, World War II heroes.

Kitty's mother, Patsy, was a Cherokee Indian. She was a starlet in the movies.

Trouble hit when Kitty was four months old. She had the measles, mumps, and chicken pox all at the same time.

When the three illnesses were over, Kitty was deaf. She could not hear at all.

Her mother knew she mustn't give in to self-pity. She had to fight this problem. And she had to bring up Kitty to fight. Kitty's mother promised herself, "My child will do the things other children do."

Patsy kept her promise. When Kitty was still a baby, her mother taught her to swim.

The family moved to Wichita Falls, Texas. At the University of Texas, Patsy learned how to teach deaf children. She got her certificate to teach.

Patsy taught many children who couldn't hear. Later, she opened the School of Listening Eyes in Wichita Falls.

Sometimes Kitty looked at other children laughing and telling secrets. She saw them singing and clapping their hands to music. Why could they hear when she couldn't?

Her mother said, "Don't think of what you *can't* do. Think of what you *can.*"

Patsy asked her if she would like to take piano lessons.

Kitty answered, "Sure."

Kitty learned to play the cello too. She couldn't hear the music, but she liked to feel the cello vibrate. Her sense of touch helped her find the right notes.

Kitty couldn't hear the shouts of children at play. She couldn't hear the radio. She didn't know what the people on TV were saying. All this made it easy for her to keep her mind on what she was doing.

By the time Kitty was eight she could play the piano and cello well.

It was very hard for Patsy to teach Kitty lip reading and speaking. Kitty had been deaf since she was a baby. She didn't know what words sounded like. But Patsy tried hard. Kitty tried too.

When she was eight, Kitty could lip read and

speak well enough to go to public school. She began in third grade.

Kitty's father was an engineer for an oil company. He flew his own plane. When Kitty was eleven, he died in a plane crash.

When she was twelve, she and her mother moved from Texas. They went to southern California. There, Kitty began to swim in meets.

Kitty saw other boys and girls diving. "I'd like to try," she told her teachers.

They told her, "You'll never be a good diver. You can't hear. Hearing and balance go together."

But only the nerve endings of the ears had been damaged when Kitty was a baby. The illness left her deaf. But it had not hurt her sense of balance.

The *Saturday Evening Post* (March 1977) tells us that one day at a swimming meet Kitty surprised her teachers. She surprised herself too. "One of our team's divers didn't show up," Kitty said. "I hardly knew one dive from another, but I asked them to let me try."

She won a gold medal at that meet. The other

divers cheered her. Kitty made up her mind. She'd work hard. She'd become a first-rate diver.

Kitty learned jackknives and half-twists. She learned back dives and cutaways. She learned half-gainers and swan dives. To do any of these, a diver needs good timing and balance. And the diver must *concentrate.* Concentrating was easy for Kitty. She'd learned when she was very young to keep her mind on what she was doing.

Six months later Kitty became the AAU Junior Olympic diving champion. Dr. Sammy Lee heard about her. Dr. Lee had won two Olympic gold medals. He asked Kitty to come to his school in Anaheim, California. He would teach her for free.

Patsy knew Kitty could be a champion diver if she tried hard. "Go to Dr. Lee's school," Patsy said.

The school wasn't easy. At first Kitty kept slapping into the water wrong—which hurts—at 40 miles an hour (64 kmph). For months she had big bruises.

Some dives from the 33-foot (10-m) platform

were very hard. Kitty had to know just when to twist in midair.

She could not hear Dr. Lee when he shouted signals. But she could sense the sound of a gunshot. Dr. Lee began using a starter's gun. It was loaded with blanks. A shot told Kitty when to twist in her dive. Kitty learned to cut the water cleanly.

Every afternoon Kitty spent four hours training. Mornings she went to Anaheim High School. Her teachers tried to keep their faces toward her. That way she could read their lips.

Sometimes they forgot. That meant Kitty had to hit the books extra hard in the evenings and on weekends. She had to make up for what she had missed in class.

Hard work didn't get Kitty down. She graduated from Anaheim High with honors. In 1963, *American Youth* magazine named her "Young American of the Month." The article about her said, "Kitty O'Neil has turned a handicap into a key to success. Deaf since she was a baby, this 16-year-old leads a very happy teen life. And she breaks one high-diving record after another. Kitty snaps up awards like a hungry fish—five trophies and fifteen gold medals so far. She is now training for the 1964 Olympics."

Kitty said, "I like to do things people say I can't do because I'm deaf. I have to work harder than some, but look at the fun I have proving they're wrong."

At the AAU Nationals, Kitty became the women's 1964 10-meter diving champion. Everyone was sure she would win a gold medal in the 1968 Olympics.

She didn't. She got spinal meningitis instead. This is a disease of the spinal cord.

Doctors said she'd never walk again.

But the doctors were wrong. Soon she was up—and looking for action.

Illness struck Kitty again when she was twenty-five. It was cancer.

She was down but not for long. She had two operations. Then she was looking for action again.

"I love to go fast and I love danger," O'Neil told a writer for the *Sun-Times Parade*.

O'Neil met Duffy Hambleton, a stunt man. They married. Kitty became a housewife. That

Kitty O'Neil will race almost anything.
She seems to thrive on challenge.

bored her. So her husband taught her to be a stunt woman.

She raced motorcycles, cars, speedboats, dune buggies, and snowmobiles. She tried skydiving, scuba diving, and hang gliding.

She water-skied and broke the world's record for women's water-skiing. She went at 104.85 mph (167 kmph).

She began competing against herself, trying to beat her own records.

She drove a three-wheeled rocket car called the Motivator. It had a horsepower of 48,000. It was made of aluminum and fiberglass and was 38 feet (11.4 m) long. It was powered by hydrogen peroxide.

The January 17, 1977, issue of *Sports Illustrated* said, "It uses hydrogen peroxide the way Niagara Falls uses water." A 600-mile-per-hour (960-kmph) run used about 100 gallons (378 l). A 5-mile (8-km) trip cost about $1,000. But there was no pollution. The only wastes were water and oxygen.

On December 4, 1976, O'Neil put on her coveralls and helmet. She roared away. Her speed

averaged 322 mph (425 kmph). She was the Fastest Woman on Earth.

On December 6, she went even faster. She averaged 512.7 mph (820.3 kmph). She tried again. She hit 618.3 mph (989.28 kmph)—only 4 miles (6.4 km) an hour under the world record held by Gary Gabelich.

Now, O'Neil earns her living as a stunt woman. She doubles for movie and TV stars. Wearing a special suit to protect her, O'Neil has been smeared with glue. Then she has been set on fire. The temperature in her suit has gone up to 93° C (200° F). Pictures are taken. The fire is then put out. O'Neil takes off the special suit. She wipes her face and smiles.

"Never give up," Kitty's mother told her when Kitty was very young. Her mother died in 1966.

In the rocket car, the Motivator,
Kitty has broken all sorts
of land speed records.

But Kitty remembers her words. And she tells people, "Keep on going. *Do* something. Don't give in."

The story of O'Neil's life was made into a program called "Silent Victory." Now Kitty herself is writing her own life story to be made into a movie. She will act in the movie too. For those who can't hear, she will have the words printed at the bottom of the screen.

O'Neil says, "I hate it when people say to me, 'You're fantastic! You're super!'"

She doesn't think she is. "I've been able to do things because I've kept on going. I haven't let trouble keep me down. I want my movie to show that."

Duffy Hambleton rolls his car during a filming of the made-for-TV movie, "The Story of Kitty O'Neil." The car rolled over eight times and was completely destroyed. Duffy walked away unharmed.

O'Neil still wants to beat the overall land speed record. She hopes to be the first woman to break the sound barrier on land. And she wants to break the overall water speed record too.

Whether she does these things or not, O'Neil has already triumphed. She didn't let anything get her down.

I told Kitty O'Neil I was writing this book. She said, "Tell your readers that handicapped is just a word. It's not a way of life."

INDEX

American Youth (magazine), 78

Amputation
  hand, 26–41
  leg, 57–70

Armes, Jay J., 26–41
  photographs of, 27, 28, 35, 39, 40

Artificial limbs. *See* Protheses

Balliett, Whitney, 17, 25

Birth defects, 1–10

Blindness, 15–25

Braille, 17

Brain damage, 42–55

Brother Ray (Charles, Ritz), 22, 23, 25

Campbell, Glen, photograph of, 18

Cancer, 57, 60, 65, 79

Casts, plaster, 61

Charles, Ray, 11–25
  photographs of, 13, 14, 18, 21

Chemotherapy, 65–67

Chicken pox, 74

Coma, 44

Crutches, 65

Deafness, 73–86

Dexter, Dave, Jr., 23

Drugs, 22, 65, 67

Ebony (magazine), 20

Education, special, 10, 53

Explosives, 30–31

Fry, Johnny, 1–10
  photograph of, 5

Gillespie, Dizzy, 23

Glaucoma, 15–16

Good Housekeeping (magazine), 63

Hambleton, Duffy, photograph of, 84

Hand amputation, 26–41

Hooks, as hand replacement, 32, 33–34, 36, 37, 38

International Valor in Sports Award, 49, 50, 53, 69, 70

Jay J. Armes, Investigator (Nolan), 31, 32

Jazz, 11, 17, 23

Jazz Story, The (Dexter), 23

John, Elton, 51
    photograph of, 52

Kennedy, Edward M., Jr., 56–70
    photographs of, 58, 62, 66, 69
Kennedy, Edward M., Sr., 56, 57, 59, 60, 67, 68, 70
    photograph of, 62
Kennedy, Joan, 56, 57, 59, 60, 67
Kennedy, John F., 56, 57
Kennedy, Robert F., 56, 57–59

Leg amputation, 57–70
Lip reading, 75, 78
Lord, Jack, photograph of, 35
Lyons, Bill, 47, 54

Mayfield, Ted, 1–6
Measles, 74
Michael, Prince of Kent, 49–51
    photograph of, 50
Miller, Kathy, 42–55
    photographs of, 43, 46, 48, 50, 52
Mumps, 74
Muscles, 32, 37, 47, 54, 61

Nerves, 47, 76
New Yorker, The (magazine), 17
Nolan, Frederick, 31, 32

Olympics, 42, 52, 53, 73, 77, 79
O'Neil, Kitty, 71–86
    photographs of, 72, 80, 82

Parachutist (magazine), 8
Peters, Mary, 51–53
Philadelphia Sportswriters Association, 54
Plaster casts, 61
Protheses, 33, 61–70

Ritz, David, 22
Rivera, Geraldo, 65

Saturday Evening Post (magazine), 76
School of Listening Eyes (Texas), 74
Silent Victory (film), 85
Soul music, 11, 15, 22
Special education, 10, 53
Special Kind of Courage, A (Rivera), 65
Spinal meningitis, 79
Sporting News (magazine), 47
Sports Illustrated (magazine), 81
State School for the Blind (Florida), 16–17
Story of Kitty O'Neil, The (TV movie), 84

Wonder Woman (TV show), 72
Wheelchairs, 64

X-rays, 60